The Art of Service:

A Collection of Haiku Poems

Lori Latimer

Published by Service of Change, LLC
© 2014 by Lori Latimer

ISBN: 978-0-9911375-6-5

www.ServiceOfChange.com

Foreword

"Small changes among the masses can have a massive impact around the world."

This is the vision behind Service of Change, a community developed by my childhood friend, Dennis Nappi II. Service of Change aims to empower us in a grass-roots effort to build innovative and caring communities. While I dedicate my professional life to supporting individuals, families, and communities as a social worker, my service doesn't end when I leave the office. That is my choice. I see beauty in our interconnection and I believe there are infinite ways to influence and implement positive change. I believe art is one of our most powerful forms of resistance and revolution. Art reflects our culture directly, holding a mirror for us to see violence, corruption, and oppression. It can make us feel vulnerable. It can make us feel defensive. At its best, art forces us to examine where we stand in the world. Am I a passive observer? Have I become cynical, and turned my back on social and political change? Or do I still believe my words and actions matter?

So my weekly contribution to the Service of Change community is a haiku. I began writing a weekly haiku in 2011, inspired by a friend and fellow change agent. While I never wrote poetry before, I was drawn to the form. I find comfort in direct communication. Simple in structure, the haiku allows me to capture the challenges and successes in our struggle to uphold our mission to be a community of helpers. Change is frightening and difficult. Service can seem thankless and hopeless. But we can find joy in the process and relief from supporting one another. Each haiku I write stems from my own experience and the people in my life who influence me in their own service of change. I do not wish lecture or preach. I only wish to be honest with you and acknowledge that our work is hard. Each week when I write my haiku, my few words send a little current of possibility through me. I want to ignite a haiku chain of revolution, seventeen syllables at a time.

Join me.

Lori Latimer, September 7, 2014

08.20.13

Each time we give back,
we set a chain reaction
of our compassion.

08.27.13

Fear and apathy
can be our worst enemies.
Fight for compassion.

09.24.13

We all make ripples.
Each act is a skipped stone –
its impact spreads wide.

10.01.13

Accept our mistakes.
Accept our differences.
Now let's compromise.

10.15.13

We get discouraged;
that's OK. It's how we know
it's time to start fresh.

10.29.13

With aggressive folks,
give them the unexpected:
empathy and calm.

11.19.13

Loving the process
without the hope for reward
will lead to great work.

12.03.13

Will you sit and watch?
Or will you stand up and act?
Which can you live with?

12.10.13

Small steps to big steps.
That's how we get to our goals.
Let us keep climbing.

12.17.13

In our fight for change,
silence is our greatest foe.
So let's now be heard.

12.24.13

If you lift someone
instead of tearing them down,
you will rise up, too.

01.07.14

Be vulnerable.
It's terrifying at first,
but you'll find your strength.

01.14.14

Exchange ideas
as we exchange currency.
Start the renaissance.

01.21.14

Let yourself receive
so you can appreciate
what it means to give.

01.28.14

Let yourself be great
in times of uncertainty.
Do not hide your gifts.

02.25.14

The words that we choose
can unify or destroy.
Use your voice for change.

03.18.14

Future and vision:
They must be a packaged deal
when you move forward.

03.25.14

When we meet new life,
it's our chance to change and grow.
It's time to start fresh.

04.08.14

It's these little acts
that let us know who we are.
What do your acts say?

04.15.14

Even if you fail,
your dream is worth your effort.
Failure trumps regret.

04.29.14

You say who you are.
Keep the naysayers at bay,
let yourself be great.

05.06.14

Heroes don't need capes,
or even super powers.
Their work is subtle.

05.13.14

When learning is shared,
discourse fosters new notions
which lead to action.

05.20.14

Persistence, patience.
We need those ingredients
to allow for change.

05.27.14

You can be in charge,
but can you be a leader?
Know the difference.

06.24.14

Fear should be embraced.
Let it push you towards growth
and great acts of change.

07.01.14

It's never too late
to find a new direction.
Your paths are endless.

About the Author:

Lori Latimer is a social worker who lives and works in Philadelphia, the city which represents her family's history. She earned her Bachelor of Arts in Comparative Literature from the University of Massachusetts at Amherst and her Master of Social Work from the University of Pennsylvania. Lori's professional background includes housing and homelessness, mental health, geriatrics, and trauma-informed care. Also, she is in love with her practices in judo and jiu jitsu, which influence Lori's writing and work.

You can connect with Lori through the following channels:

Follow her on Twitter:

@LoriLatimer1

Read her personal blog, Uphill:

http://www.latattack.wordpress.com

Service of Change, LLC

"Small changes among the masses can have a massive impact around the world."

Be The Change!

www.ServiceOfChange.com

www.ingramcontent.com/pod-product-compliance
Lightning Source LLC
Chambersburg PA
CBHW060716030426
42337CB00017B/2887